FAYE A

A STORY THAT OFFERS UNDENIABLE
PROOF OF LIFE AFTER DEATH

A **FAX** FROM HEAVEN

Revised Edition

A FAX FROM HEAVEN
Revised in 2024

© Copyright 2012 – Faye Aldridge

DAVIS JACKSON PUBLISHERS
311 DUDLEY LANE
LEBANON, TN 37087

(615) 444-7332

Library of Congress control number 2009912357

ISBN 978-0-988-74288-8

Contents

Are after-death appearances possible according
to the Bible? Scripture verses in Matthew 17:1-3
tell us after-death appearances are indeed possible.

Moses had been dead for some 1500 years,
and Elijah, had been absent from earth 800
years when they met with Jesus on the holy
mountain known as the Mt. of Transfiguration.
Eyewitnesses saw Moses and Elijah with Jesus
and heard them talking. They were alive and
well at the Lord's transfiguration.

Are all after-death appearances from God?
We would be foolish to suppose that Satan
would not disguise himself as an angel of
light or send some of his servants back
to deceive and mislead those who do not
possess discernment. Perhaps we should
question the outcome of each visit.

In reference to A FAX FROM HEAVEN,
both the deceased and his widow were
born again believers, saved by the blood
of Jesus, when the after-death visits occurred.
With that in mind, I do believe we are
safe to assume the story is true and
sent by God, since it was confirmed by two
highly credible witnesses.

Readers from all over the world have read
A FAX FROM HEAVEN, and the book has
generally been recognized, as a gift of hope,
inspiring readers to seek the Lord Jesus,
while there is time.

CHAPTER 1

A Fax from Heaven

A Nashville oncologist was stunned when a deceased patient appeared in his living room and spoke to him. Later, Dr. Carl Willis learned he was not the only physician who experienced an after-death appearance from Burke Aldridge. The following paragraph is an excerpt taken from a letter written by Dr. Willis, soon after the other-worldly experience.

> "Every once in a while, something happens to you that you just can't explain. You know, when all you can do is take pause or stand still in complete awe...that night between 11:30 and 12:00, as I sat alone on the couch in my family room, something happened. Initially I was frightened and uneasy,

only to be overcome, just as suddenly, by a sense of peace and calmness like I have never known before. There was a translucent form there, which I did not recognize. Then I heard a voice, which I had heard before, say, 'I have gone to Heaven to be with God. Don't worry about me, I am OK.' I knew that voice. I didn't need to call the hospital to find out that Mr. Aldridge had gone on to be with God, just as he had said."

My husband, Burke, had been under a physician's care for months. Suffering from continuous pain had become a way of life for him, but the source of the pain remained a mystery. On a cold February night in 2005, I rushed him to the emergency room at Baptist Hospital in Nashville, Tennessee. His pain had reached an unbearable level and was accompanied by acute respiratory distress.

The emergency staff responded at once when they realized the severity of Burke's symptoms. His right lung had collapsed. Within minutes, the nurse started him on oxygen and administered an injection of morphine to lessen the severe chest pain. The attending physician then admitted Burke to the critical care unit, a unit reserved for only the most life-threatening conditions.

For the next five days, medical professionals examined, probed, biopsied, scanned, and X-rayed Burke's body relentlessly. His pain never decreased and his inability to breathe became nearly unbearable. It was hard to believe this critically ill man had been busy living an active life only days before. Now my strong, 53-year-old husband slipped in and out of consciousness, engaged in a battle for his life.

I did all I could to make him comfortable. He knew how much I loved him, and I assured him that I would remain by his side. I prayed for him, and I read Scripture to him even when he was not conscious. I knew his spirit had to remain strong in order to fight the attack against his body.

On the sixth day, the biopsy results confirmed the worst: Burke had lung cancer, and it had spread to his spine. He was in the fourth and final stage with a life expectancy of only 30 days. Burke calmly listened to the ominous prognosis, then looked at me and said, "Where is the fear? It's strange but there is no fear." I understood and agreed with him because I was also free of fear.

We both knew God was with us in the midst of the chaos and we were extremely grateful for His presence.

How do you tell your children you are dying? How do you find the right words?

As a father, Burke was outstanding. From day one, he participated in the care of our son and daughter, David and Donna. When they were babies, he rocked them to sleep and fed them almost as often as I did. When they were young children, he nurtured them and played games with them. He spent quality time with each child, patiently listening to questions and answering in ways they could understand. Burke had the unique ability to see life through their eyes, never expecting them to see life through his. As the children grew, they often sang and played guitar with their dad. Our family loved sincerely, laughed frequently, and we were openly affectionate. We were happy together, and saying good-bye would prove to be the hardest thing, we had ever done.

The evening after we had received the doctor's prognosis, our children arrived at the hospital. I sat nearby and listened as Burke told them the dreadful news. A feeling of helplessness came over me as I watched them attempt to control their emotions.

Tears welled in their eyes and spilled over in silence as they tried to be strong for their dad. We had never experienced that kind of pain before. I could almost hear their hearts breaking. I felt as if a part of me was dying.

It was Burke's nature to find the good in any situation, a quality that did not fail him even in that terrible moment of realization. Gently, Burke told the children how wonderful it was to love them, to be their dad, and to have shared their lives with them. He spoke plainly to them of the importance of faith in our Lord. He reminded them to look past this temporary life toward the approaching life eternal, where the word good-bye does not exist. He expressed his desire that God would use the situation and cause something good to come from his premature death.

It was late when David and Donna went home. I settled down in a chair, wanting to sleep—to escape reality. Burke's breathing was difficult. He was in excruciating pain and restless in the unfamiliar hospital bed. It was a time filled with bittersweet emotions. We all lived through that day, but I believe it was the most heartrending day we ever endured.

The following days and nights turned into a blur of continuous mental and physical anguish. Family and friends came for brief visits. They came to say good-bye to a very deserving and special person whose life appeared to be drawing to a close. Outside the door, they wept and then dried their eyes before entering the room.

Burke bravely faced his last days, though weary from relentless pain and the ever-present struggle to breathe. He described his intense pain as half-physical and half-heartsick pain. Leaving his loved ones caused him great distress. As others hid their tears, so did I. I hid them well in an attempt to spare him even more pain. He could not bear to think of leaving me alone, so I pretended I was a rock even when I felt like a pebble.

The morning of February 28, day 22 of Burke's final journey, began with a fine, cold rain. Gray clouds hovered over the city. I stood by his bed watching him sleep and listening to each breath. He was heavily sedated. For the moment, I was thankful he was not hurting.

Suddenly, Burke's eyes opened and he smiled a radiant smile. He was wide-awake when he told me he had been with the Lord. He said the Lord had showed him things of Heaven and spoke to him about them. With great peace, Burke told me, "The Lord said I can come home and He will help me cross over." My husband reminded me that his quality of life had diminished to the point where he was no longer living, merely existing in agony. With no hesitation and an unmistakable anticipation, Burke told me he was ready to go. I could no longer hide my tears, and they fell down my face. He smiled at me and said, "No regrets." My heart was breaking, but I nodded and agreed, "No regrets."

I did not give up at that time, but I did give in. I accepted God's will. I knew Burke was in God's hands, and I had done all I could do. My prayers changed; I no longer prayed for Burke to stay on earth. I promised him I would remain beside him and hold his hand until Jesus took his other hand to lift him up to Heaven. He assured me that he would meet me there when it was my turn to cross over.

In a short time, the Lord allowed me to keep my promise; I held Burke's hand as his life on earth ended later that same day. Death came for him just before midnight. As I held Burke's hand in mine, I became aware of a magnificent, holy presence. Although it was beyond my physical sight, I knew that a heavenly presence saturated the very atmosphere of the room. There was a strong feeling of anticipation in the air as Burke's spirit left his body. If I had reached above my head, I believe I could have touched the angels. In my spirit, I could hear them rejoicing, "Burke's coming home... Burke's coming home!" I found comfort in the knowledge that his life in Heaven was about to begin.

I called our children after Burke died, and they came to say good-bye. We left the hospital just before three o'clock in the morning as giant, unpredicted snowflakes blanketed the streets. Snow was not in the forecast; however, Burke had repeatedly mentioned seeing snow the day before. Against the wishes of the children, I drove home alone. I had to reconcile within my heart the reality of my situation.

My strength was gone. Exhaustion and loneliness overwhelmed me. I could hardly see the road because the snowfall was very heavy. It took me almost an hour to get to our home in the country. Darkness accentuated the lonely music made by wind chimes swaying in the cold, winter wind.

I drove into the garage and pressed the remote, closing the garage door. It closed partially then raised right back up. It closed successfully on the second try.

I did not think it was significant until the same thing happened the next two nights when I entered the garage. Each time, it was as if someone walked into the garage behind me, triggering the safety device. I saw no one.

I slept about three hours before David came over at 8 a.m. As soon as he arrived, the phones began to ring. David answered but heard only a dial tone. The ringing continued as he moved from phone to phone all through the house. The answering machine was set to answer after four rings; however, the answering machine did not respond, though it was in perfect working condition. All the phones in the house were ringing. The ringing stopping after a dozen rings. Suddenly, I remembered—Burke said he was going to try to send me a fax when he got to Heaven letting me know he was all right. I said as much to David. He bounded up the stairs to my office and discovered the fax machine was unplugged. We shook our heads in uncertainty, wondering what just happened.

Two days later, Dr. Arthur Cushman, a neurosurgeon, and his wife, Carolyn, visited our family at the funeral home. Dr. Cushman called me aside and told me a miraculous, unusual report—Burke had appeared in his home the night before, nearly 24 hours after his death. He said Burke appeared to him in the center of a white light. He described what he saw: "Burke's body was surrounded by a white light like a white halo. He looked very healthy and happy and appeared to be younger than at the time of his death."

Burke spoke to him saying, "Don't worry, Slim, I'm all right." (Slim was a nickname Burke had called him for many years.) Dr. Cushman continued, "He then gradually faded out of sight. There was no one else with him, but I could tell he was in a beautiful land filled with flowers; I could see the flowers behind him. This is the only time I have ever had an experience like that. I surely am glad that Burke came to tell me good-bye."

My family and I welcomed the news as a rare gift of hope from God. We knew Burke was a Christian and we believed he was in Heaven. The news of Burke's after-death appearance to Dr. Cushman was a welcome source of encouragement. My family and I gained strength when we learned of the encounter. Amazement and appreciation filled me in response to the Lord's generous gift. I sensed that God was reminding me, "I am with you; you are never alone."

Days later, I had a conversation with Dr. Willis, Burke's oncologist. He, too, had a story to tell. He told me Burke visited him in his home on the very night he died. Dr. Willis reported he was in his family room reading a book that night. He saw something unusual in his peripheral vision—a shimmering white light. As he refocused his eyes, the light began to manifest into the shape of a man's body. Dr. Willis could not clearly see the man's face because the man was translucent. Dr. Willis was astounded when he heard Burke's voice say, "I have gone to Heaven to be with God. Don't worry about me. I am OK."

Dr. Willis said in a letter to me, "I knew that voice. I didn't need to call the hospital to find out that Mr. Aldridge had gone on to be with God, just as he had said. He was ready for the Lord, and the Lord was ready for him, despite my intentions. I think he must have known how much I wanted to help him, and he stopped by just to let me know he was feeling a whole lot better. He was breathing a lot better and he had no more pain. He had met a better Doctor who had given him rest and comfort and had granted him everlasting life. I hope this recap of my encounter brings comfort to you."

I asked Dr. Willis and Dr. Cushman for written documentation of the encounters. Both physicians were kind enough to comply with my request. Dr. Cushman faxed a letter to me on March 29, 2005, and Dr. Willis faxed his letter to me on March 31, 2005. I sat at my desk reading the letters and contemplating the significance of the content. I smiled as I realized the true meaning of the letters. I really did get a fax from Heaven. The message that I received from Burke by way of two physicians was, "I've gone to Heaven to be with God. Don't worry. I am OK." Two witnesses confirmed the message.

This true story was further authenticated by a televised interview with the two doctors who witnessed the after-death appearances and a news report conducted by Jennifer Johnson, news anchor for WSMV Channel 4 News of Nashville, Tennessee. This televised segment documented the testimonies of Dr. Carl Willis and Dr. Arthur Cushman, both from the Nashville area. In the interview, the physicians stated they personally witnessed an otherworldly, apparition in their respective homes shortly after Burke Aldridge died of cancer at Baptist Hospital in Nashville.

The interview is accessible at:
https://www.youtube.com/watch?v=iAYtqgcZC8k

> And we know that God causes all
> things to work together for good to
> those who love God, to those who
> are called according to His purpose.
> *Romans 8:28*

NOTE: This is an after-thought but I believe it is significant enough to mention. During the six months prior to Burke's death, he experienced a recurring dream on numerous occasions. Each time, his deceased grandmother came to him asking him the same question.

She asked, "Burke, are you ready to go?" His reply was always the same. "Not yet, Gran," to which she replied, "I'll be back." The visual aspect of the dream was identical each time and the communication was the same.

Each time, Burke seemed a bit puzzled by the dream and the increased frequency of the occurrences. It makes a lot of sense now, looking back on the circumstances. Gran was preparing him for the transition. In my mind, this is additional proof for my strong belief that many dreams are heavenly forms of communication.

CHAPTER 2

A Yellow Rose

I carried two large bags of groceries from the garage into the kitchen. The house was quiet. A miniature pink rose rested on the counter of the island in the center of our kitchen. A small square of folded white paper sat behind the beautiful rose. I picked up the note and smiled as I read: *"To say I love you would be enough, I know; but I'd rather say 'I love you' with a rose."* The note was signed, *"Love, Burke."*

I placed the rose in a small vase of water, tucked the little note in my wallet between my library and voter registration cards, and in a few days I forgot about the heartwarming little gift.

I absolutely love flowers and they were a recurring theme in our marriage; beginning with the beautiful gardenias that filled the church on the day of our wedding. The fragrance of the gardenia is sweet, aromatic, and unmistakable. Many times, I have placed a gardenia blossom or a rose bud on my pillow just so I could enjoy the wonderful fragrance as I drifted off to sleep.

Burke gave me flowers on many occasions during our marriage—sometimes roses, sometimes Stargazer lilies; however, he knew yellow roses were my favorite. I always thanked my husband and carried on over his lovely flower gifts. In hindsight, I never appreciated them enough.

My husband died a few months after he gave me the sweet little miniature rose.

In the days that followed Burke's death, flowers came pouring into the funeral home and the church; some were delivered to our home. Words could never express the depths of my gratitude; each flower meant someone was remembering Burke and that fact deeply touched my heart. Three cherished words echoed in my mind each time a floral arrangement was delivered; I suppose as long as I live, flowers will always mean "I love you" to me.

After Burke's funeral, I took many of the beautiful, fresh flowers to my home. All too soon, the colorful flowers withered and died. When there were no more fresh flowers in the house, I missed them a great deal.

Three weeks after I buried my husband, the florist delivered a unique arrangement to my home. There were so many fresh flowers. The arrangement was nearly three feet high. I have never seen such a gorgeous array. The square, ivory-colored-metal container held a fabulous assortment of all kinds of flowers. Purple iris and yellow roses were predominant; they stood out strikingly above all the rest. I opened the envelope that accompanied the flowers to find my friend, Charline Wilhite, had sent them. She waited to send her gift in memory of Burke, knowing that it would be even more special after all the others had faded and died. I positioned the arrangement in the center of my long dining table, in front of the kitchen fireplace.

Each morning I sat in the kitchen, sipping my coffee next to an empty chair, trying to adapt to a new way of life. Every time I glanced at the flowers, I received a bit of comfort. The floral bouquet conveyed three familiar words to my heart: "I love you." I am quite certain that Charline never realized how much her gift meant to me during the early days of adjustment, although I did express my gratitude.

As the days passed, one by one, the flowers drooped and died. Each day, I removed the dead ones, leaving the live ones in ample water. Finally, the day came when all the flowers were gone. Only the greenery remained alive, except for one yellow rose. I stopped adding water to the container, but, surprisingly, the gorgeous, perfectly formed little rose did not droop and it did not fade. After a month, I removed the rose from the greenery and laid it on the mantle.

Though the rose remained on the mantle for many weeks and became dry to the touch, the color remained vibrant, its head never drooped, and the petals never withered. Thinking the little yellow rose must have been treated with a preservative; I carried it with me and visited the florist to find what they had done to make it stay so perfect. Each employee looked at it and admired the rose, but no one had an explanation. The floral shop owner said he had never seen a rose remain so perfectly preserved. He remarked, "Only God could do such a thing." He suggested I store it in a sealed glass container for preservation.

One day, I was sorting out the contents of my wallet and a folded, square piece of white paper fell out. I picked it up and unfolded it. Once again I read, "To say I love you would be enough, I know; but I'd rather say 'I love you' with a rose. Love, Burke." Could it be? He had been in Heaven for months. Was the unusual little rose his way of saying, "I love you"?

Many years have passed and the little rose remains the same—its vibrant, yellow petals are fully opened and the stem is still green.

Since Burke died, I have learned to accept the gifts and not question the Giver. I hear Him say, "I love you" each time I look at the extraordinary yellow rose that never died.

CHAPTER 3

Slow Motion

When I was a child growing up in rural Mississippi, I was involved in a very serious car accident. I was only ten years old when my mother assigned the chore of grocery shopping to me one Saturday morning. At that early age, I knew what to buy and what not to buy, and I made no exceptions. We had very little money. My father died at the age of 25 leaving three children under the age of five to be cared for by my mother. We did not own a car and town was two miles away. The man who owned the land where we lived and worked offered me a ride that morning.

I rode in the back seat of Mr. Landrum's new Plymouth, and I don't remember saying a word on the trip to town. My list was short and simple; I completed the shopping and placed the groceries in the trunk of the car for the ride home. My grandmother who lived near us rode in the back seat with me, and a cousin rode on the front seat with Mr. Landrum.

Central Mississippi is mostly flat land; however, there was a hill on the outskirts of town to the north. We began our descent down that hill, and something frightening happened. The car swerved from one side of the road to the other. I recall Mr. Landrum yelling, "I can't steer it. It won't stop." The car careened from one shoulder of the road to the other as it picked up speed going down the hill approaching the bridge that spanned Box's Creek. Strangely and fortunately, there were no other cars in sight.

There were no seat belts to restrain us, so we pitched from side to side as the car approached the bridge abutments of Box's Creek Bridge. The road was built up high to protect it from the creek overflow during heavy rains and that elevation created an element of danger.

Just before we reached the bridge abutment, Mr. Landrum overcompensated and turned the steering wheel hard to the left. We missed the bridge abutment and made a complete U-turn, which led us to the edge of the road where we began our descent. The car rolled over repeatedly until it came to rest against a row of trees and a barbed wire fence adjacent to a cotton field.

Divine intervention surely saved us. First, there were no other cars in sight so that eliminated the possibility of a head-on collision. Second, we did not hit the solid concrete bridge abutment that would have caused devastation. Third, we received no injuries in the wreck. God demonstrated His power as He protected us that day. God left evidence of His presence in the mind of a child. I remember how the car made a complete revolution several times, yet we did not crash against the glass or metal, as we logically should have. Mysteriously, God enclosed us in a safe place within the car. He surrounded us with a hedge of protection, in the form of sparkling particles of white light.

From the moment we left the road, life changed. Time was somehow altered. The distortion did not halt the wreck. The accident still took place, only it happened in slow motion. Inside the car on that particular day, we appeared to be weightless and the laws of gravity no longer seemed to apply. I felt no fear or distress as my body tumbled in unison with the tumbling automobile. I was not injured when my head slowly landed against the ceiling of the car as it rolled over and over.

I distinctly remember seeing small, sparkling particles of white light swirling before my curious eyes. The lights were everywhere, all around us. My mind focused on the tiny light particles. I saw each one separately as one sees snowflakes drifting separately on a snowy winter day. Each tiny particle of light appeared to be unique and different. I was calm, and my thoughts were simply 'wow, wow, and wow'.

When the car landed upright, we managed to crawl out of it even though the top was crushed. We walked away unharmed.

In recent days, I have heard others speak of seeing the same sparkling particles of white light in times of crisis. It seems the light particles have the ability to separate into tiny sparkling particles or cluster together, taking shape as angelic beings, an obvious halo or one solid mass of white light. This explanation is conceivable for what I saw and experienced during the accident. The holy particles of light surrounded us that day, as plentiful as feathers in a pillow. They protected us from injuries in a wreck that logically should have killed everyone inside the car.

> The angel of the Lord encamps around those who fear Him, and rescues them.
> *Psalm 34:7*

CHAPTER 4

More Than a Dream

Autumn finally arrived. My husband, Burke, and I busied ourselves working and preparing to go out of state for a weeklong business convention. Our two children, Donna and David, were in elementary school, but we arranged for them to leave school for one week. We planned to drive them to the home of Burke's parents in central Mississippi. The kids would stay there while we flew from Jackson, Mississippi, to the West Coast.

Two weeks before our departure date, I had an unsettling dream. The details of the dream lingered vividly in my mind. In the dream, I was a spectator. I usually dreamed in color; however, that time was in black and white. I stood at a distance from the scene watching the circumstances unfold, as one would watch a ball game from the bleachers. I was not capable of entering the scene by speaking or walking into it; I could only stand by and watch.

The first thing I saw was a woman standing with her back toward me. She appeared to be me. She looked upward at a small box. The box appeared to be suspended in mid-air, as if an invisible hand supported it.

I watched as the woman wept; she dropped to her knees and fell forward to where her face was against the ground. Forcefully, she struck the ground with her hands and she cried as if her heart would break.

I felt her pain. Her cries became my cries, and her grief became my grief. I ached and I was certain that we were experiencing the same emotions. I looked intently at the suspended box. I trembled when I realized it was not just a box; it was a small casket. Strangely, I knew the woman's child was in that casket. Emotion overwhelmed me when I believed I was watching myself in a premonition. Somehow, I experienced grief, brokenness, and a sense of helplessness. I had never felt anything like that in my entire life.

The dream faded away, and I awoke literally shivering. I quietly made my way down the hall to David and Donna's bedrooms. I gently brushed their cheeks with kisses as they slept, thanking God they were safe in their beds. I went back and forth from room to room. I did not want to let either of them out of my sight.

I assumed I had a nightmare. I told my husband about the dream the next day, and explained I felt like it was some kind of warning to safeguard the kids even more than we usually did. Somehow, I knew it was more than a dream. In my heart, I felt it was symbolic of what was to come in the days ahead.

Two weeks passed, and we were indecisive about canceling the trip. The children were healthy, happy, and looking forward to the long visit with their grandparents. The plane tickets were in hand. I told myself I was silly to let a dream affect me that way. We decided to go ahead with our plans.

On Sunday night, we arrived at our destination and checked into our hotel. I could not shake the sense of impending danger. We made it through Monday and my apprehension grew stronger. A gentle pressure invaded my thinking, and the pressure did not let up. My husband shared my apprehension by that time, and he insisted that we should cancel the week and fly to Mississippi the next day, and we did.

We arrived at the home of my in-laws the next evening, and we gathered our children in our arms. On Wednesday, we drove home to Tennessee. Thursday morning, our work schedules returned to normal. I was in my office when I received a phone call from my sister in Mobile. I placed the phone receiver to my ear and I heard Barbara call my name. The dream vividly played again in my mind as I heard her say the words, "Ashley is dead." Once again, I saw that small box clearly and dreadfully. The terrible pain I felt two weeks before in the dream besieged me as I listened to the agony in my sister's voice. She told me their 13-month-old daughter just drowned in Marie's backyard pool.

While Barbara worked, her best friend Marie cared for Ashley. Ashley began walking when she was nine months old. She was a beautiful baby with golden curls, sparkling blue eyes, and a constant smile. On the day of the accident, Marie thought her son was with Ashley and her son thought his mom was with Ashley. That beloved baby girl slipped out of their sight and made her way straight to the pool. She loved to be near the water. When they realized she was missing, it was too late.

We drove to Mobile that same day to be with my sister, her husband, and their young son. I ached inside for the loss of that little angel. When we arrived, I did all I could, but I could do nothing that made a difference. Ashley's toys, clothes, and photographs were evidence throughout the house that she once lived there. My beautiful little niece was gone. The absence of her sweet baby talk left her loved ones speechless and heartbroken. She was buried in a casket like the one in the dream.

Later, I tried to sort out the dream details. The woman in the dream looked like me; so does my sister. In hindsight, I saw what I should have done. I wish I had called my sister and warned her to take extra precautions with Ashley. Perhaps she would have insisted that Marie fix the gate to the pool instead of just asking her to fix the gate that day. I did not know about the broken gate lock, but my sister did. If only I had shared the dream. I believed the woman in the dream was me. I never imagined the woman in the dream was my sister.

At that time in my life, I knew about God; however, I did not know God. There is a big difference. I did not have a personal relationship with Jesus Christ. I knew about Heaven and hell, but I did not fully comprehend either. I accepted Jesus as my Savior as a child, but I lived separated from God in much of my adult life. Even though I prayed during those times, I did not know the meaning of faith, so praying was awkward and empty. I received little comfort when I prayed. Those days were difficult to say the least.

As a Christian today, I realize Jesus or His angel lifted that innocent baby girl from the pool that day. Surely, He carried her straight to Heaven. I cannot change circumstances, but I wish I could. What I can do now, is acknowledge messages and warnings from God when they come. They come in the form of dreams, visions, and spiritual prompting. I believe they come by way of the Holy Spirit. They are real godly gifts sent for a reason—and should never be ignored.

> Then they said to him, "We have had a dream and there is no one to interpret it." Then Joseph said to them, "Do not interpretations belong to God?"
> *Genesis 40:8*

CHAPTER 5

Faith

PART I

In the springtime of 1994, I was a committed Christian and had been for three years. I accepted Jesus at the age of ten and received baptism at that time. As an adult, I wandered away from the Lord, attempting to live life by my own wisdom. That did not work out very well.

My true conversion to Christianity came in 1991 along with the sincere desire to seek the Lord with all my heart.

> Then you will call upon Me and come and pray to Me, and I will listen to you. You will seek Me and find Me when you search for Me with all your heart.
> *Jeremiah 29:12-13*

During that period, I developed an intense desire to read God's Word, the Bible. As I sought the Lord each morning, by way of His Word, my comprehension of faith increased and God tested my faith as the Bible teaches us He will do.

I experienced trials and tribulations after committing my life to Jesus. There were times when I felt God's presence in ways that simply astounded me. I discovered God was always with me in the midst of enormous trials.

Our daughter, Donna, became very ill only six months after her first son was born. She developed an inflammatory disease that affected her whole body. Donna's physical condition did not improve with time and prayer. She sought medical attention from a physician but despite his efforts, her health deteriorated. We continued to pray for God to heal her.

March 24, 1994, is a memorable date. That night, I received an unforgettable message from the Lord in the form of a vision, and I believe God sent the vision to help strengthen our faith for the difficult days ahead with the illness our daughter faced.

The Divine experience began as a dream while I was sound asleep. The occurrence continued after I awoke and sat straight up in bed, fully conscious.

Indeed God speaks once, or twice, yet no one notices it. In a dream, a vision of the night, when sound sleep falls on men, while they slumber in their beds, then He opens the ears of men, and seals their instruction. *Job 33:14-16*

In the dream portion of the vision, I saw a very old ship with hoisted sails full of the stormy wind that caused the sea to lap at the ship's hull. Powerful waves tossed the vessel back and forth. I saw a heavy anchor beneath the water's surface holding the ship securely in place. I possessed total comprehension of the ship above and below. I was able to see every portion of the ship as if I had a thousand eyes, positioned above, below, and all around, viewing every inch of the ship's body simultaneously. Trying to remember that particular ability is frustrating because that ability is incomprehensible and impossible for me as a human. In the vision, God allowed me to experience that unusual comprehension during the vision.

I watched the ship while it was anchored in the storm; the anchor held it firmly. An invisible hand lifted the anchor and the ship tossed violently, in every direction. When the invisible hand lowered the anchor, the ship rocked but weathered the storm.

When the visual aspect of the experience progressed, I heard a genderless monotone voice. The holy voice spoke Scriptures that I recognized immediately from the first chapter of the Book of James. The voice said, "When you pray, ask in faith, without doubting; to doubt is like a ship being tossed by the waves of the sea." When the anchor held the ship steady, I comprehended that was *faith*. When an invisible power raised the anchor, and the ship tossed in uncertainty, I perceived that was *doubt*.

> But if any of you lacks wisdom, let him ask of God, who gives to all generously and without reproach, and it will be given to him. But he must ask in faith without any doubting, for the one who doubts is like the surf of the sea, driven and tossed by the wind. For that man ought not to expect that he will receive anything from the Lord, being a double-minded man, unstable in all his ways. *James 1:5-8*

The night vision ended when I was sitting up, fully awake.

I went back to sleep, and the entire vision, including the spoken message, repeated until I sat wide-awake for the second time. I went to sleep again, and the entire vision episode repeated a third time. As I sat up in bed, I noticed it was five o'clock in the morning. I felt like I had just returned from an exhausting trip to an unfamiliar place.

I reached over and gently touched my husband's shoulder, shaking him awake. I did not try to describe the unusual occurrence because it was too complex to explain in detail. I simply said, "God is preparing us. Something is coming, and I don't know what. We are going to have to trust God and hold onto our faith."

Less than 24 hours later, Donna landed in the emergency room at Nashville Memorial Hospital. She experienced severe unrelenting pain that forced her to seek help. Our daughter underwent a series of diagnostic studies. One of the scans revealed a tumor in her left lung. Ever present was an inflammatory process that affected her from the top of her head to the soles of her feet; she suffered greatly.

Days later, a pulmonary specialist performed a bronchoscopy in an attempt to get a biopsy of the lung tumor. The doctor was not successful in his attempt because of the location of the tumor. Donna regained consciousness following that procedure then suffered a vagus spasm. As a result, her pulse disappeared and her heartbeat faded as she lapsed into unconsciousness. The medical team responded quickly, and Donna began breathing normally again in minutes.

Donna's body was physically exhausted. She was emotionally drained. Following that frightening episode, she refused further treatment. Her doctor recommended that she have surgery to remove the tumor from the lung. She refused to have the surgery, explaining that she would trust God to heal her. She agreed to go on medication that helped decrease the widespread inflammation and pain.

Against his better judgment, the doctor agreed to abide by her wishes. He had no choice so he suggested she have an X-ray every three months, then every six months to monitor lung changes. I remember the doctor said, "If you live six years, we will know the tumor is not cancer. If you were my daughter, I would insist that you have the surgery at once." She thanked him and declined. I supported her decision because of the vision. I believed God sent the vision as encouragement. To me, it indicated we were to face the matter by trusting the Lord, walking through the affliction by faith.

Many years have passed since that trying time and Donna has lived a normal life since then. So what happened? I can only believe the vision was God's way of conveying to us that life is survivable when we walk by faith without any doubting. It was a time of testing.

> Beloved, do not be surprised at the fiery ordeal among you, which comes upon you for your testing, as though some strange thing were happening to you.
> *First Peter 4:12*

The repetition of the vision to me was confirmation that it was a true vision like the one sent to the Apostle Peter as described in the Book of Acts, the tenth chapter. Peter received a vision from the Lord and this happened to him three times. Peter was perplexed in mind as to what the vision might mean. The repetition also led me to believe Donna's illness would be prolonged and she would not be healed overnight. I surmised that persistent and unwavering faith would be required to endure it. Donna was not healed in an instant. She was healed over a prolonged period, as the tumor decreased in size. God granted her the ability to live in spite of her physical affliction. (I do not recommend the route Donna chose to anyone who reads this.) Each individual should respond based on his or her own level of faith, professional medical advice and particular set of circumstances.

Through the years and the trials, I have discovered that life is not always easy. We survive the trials with God's help. He is with us in the good times and the bad times.

> *...The Lord is my helper, I will not be afraid... Hebrews 13:6*

PART 2

Nearly twenty years later, I sat reading a book called Dark Night of the Soul by Saint John of the Cross. I began reading about the Seven Holy Virtues also known as the Seven Moral Virtues. They are faith, hope, love, prudence, justice, fortitude and temperance.

An amazing feeling came over me as I read about the first and second Virtues of faith and hope. The description of faith and hope in John's words got my full attention. Here is what I read.

Faith involves ardent belief in God and His Word. One of the early Christian symbols for faith is a ship, which represents the Church of Jesus Christ, a vessel that carries Christians safely through life into the next life.

Hope takes a positive view of the future, and it believes that the goodness of God will prevail over all forms of evil and darkness. The early Christian symbol for hope is an anchor, which contains a hidden cross. [1]

I closed my eyes, trying to recall every single detail of the vision after reading the significance of the ship and the anchor. The vision I experienced in 1994 made even more sense in 2012 after reading about the early Christian symbols. I realized the vision had a two-fold meaning and a delayed effect. God waited years to reveal that to me.

The message in 1994 was all about faith and endurance, without any doubting. God was teaching me that faith is real and touchable. You and I can stand

[1]

on it when we have nowhere else to turn and it will not fail us. That is when we 'just stand' and believe although circumstances and people may tell us to give up and walk away.

The ship in the vision was a reminder that faith is the vessel that will takes us through to the next life. The anchor in the vision was a reminder that hope is the anchor for the soul, both sure and steadfast. We can trust the anchor to hold when our world seems destructible or out of control.

The hidden cross in the anchor was a reminder that by faith in Jesus Christ, we have hope in all things. Hope in this fragile and temporary life and hope imperishable in the heavenly realm that awaits us when we die.

The vision invigorated me all over again as it did so many years ago. It was remarkable that God sent me those reminders precisely when He did. It just so happened that I was praying and believing for many needs for many loved ones. Some of my prayer requests were so complex that they seemed impossible to achieve. Failure to receive the answers to certain prayers meant loved ones might remain lost. So much was at stake that I could not entertain the thought of giving up.

For quite some time, I had felt like I was standing on a stepping-stone in the middle of the ocean. Winds of doubt came blowing in at times, whispering discouragement, telling me to give up. The Lord knew exactly what I needed to reinforce my faith.

My faith was renewed. I knew what I had to do. I had to stand firm, believing, praising and trusting. The ship, the anchor and the cross sent a message to my spirit, saying, 'Never give up.' I knew then, every answer would come in God's timing. Not some answers but every single answer to every single prayer. All I had to do was 'just stand'. After all, I was praying for those people because I loved them. The Holy Spirit gave me one more nudge, reminding me,

"Love never fails."
First Corinthians 13:8

CHAPTER 6

His Ways

God made the heavens, the earth, and the universe. I have no doubt that He spoke light into existence and created the sun, moon, and stars. It is easy for me to accept the awesome might and power of God with the faith of a child.

However, I suppose the ways of the Lord in the details of life will seem foreign to me as long as I am on this side of Heaven. His concern over the small details of life will always amaze and delight me. Why would Almighty God bother Himself with the seemingly trivial or insignificant things—little things, such as an earring?

My husband and I prepared to leave town early one morning. The car was packed, and I had just fastened the clasp on my wristwatch and put on my earrings. I turned to walk out of the bedroom and I heard a quiet, divine voice say, "Go, and look in the mirror." I paused for a moment questioning why I should receive such instruction, and then did as the voice had directed me. I turned on the light and looked closely at myself in the mirror. Then I saw it. One earring was an ordinary white pearl and the other was a silver ball.

With a smile and a bit of wonder I said, "Thank You, Lord."

Would it have mattered if I had worn mismatched earrings? Certainly not. I would have been annoyed by the mistake, but it really would not have mattered in the end. However, for some reason, it mattered to the Lord.

That kind of Divine intervention is puzzling yet pleasing to me. I am so thankful that God notices everything. I just do not know why He bothers. The fact remains that He does; and I love Him for it.

I remember one summer when everyone in my family had too much going on in their lives. They were always gone from home and I ended up cutting the grass until late one evening. The house was empty and quiet when I finished working in the yard and headed in for a shower. Just as I entered the bedroom, I heard a holy voice say, "Kneel and pray." I received no instruction as to what I should pray, but I obeyed. I stepped toward the side of the bed and dropped to my knees. I prayed and thanked God for our blessings. I remained there a moment, just waiting for further direction, but I heard nothing else.

As I arose from my kneeling position, I turned my head to the left and looked toward the floor. A huge spider scurried off the leg of my jeans and onto the carpet. I killed the spider with my shoe. I remember thanking God for showing me the spider before it bit me or got under the bed. He knew my dislike for spiders, and once again, He was watching over me.

One more story.

One morning, after working in the flowerbed on the side of our home, I was alone in the house and walking though the upstairs hall. A Holy Voice distinctly said, "Look out the window." I walked to the nearest window and looked out over the flowerbed. I admired the freshly cut grass and the shade provided by the two tall hickory trees in the yard; but I was puzzled by that long, straight, black stick near the flower bed. I was sure I had cleaned up all the debris around the flowerbed, and the stick should not have been there.

At that moment, the long, black stick began to crawl and slither from side to side until it ended up in the flowerbed. It was a very long, black snake. I dislike snakes and avoid them if possible. When my husband returned home, he searched until he found the snake, then he carried it off by the tail. The snake was not poisonous, but it was still a snake. Once again, the Lord protected me.

How could we ever doubt God about anything? He is all-powerful, full of love, mercy and forgiveness. The Lord sees all and knows all there is to know about each one of us. He is in charge and all we have to do is follow His rules and be obedient.

He keeps up with the entire universe and He knows when I am wearing mismatched earrings and warns me about spiders and snakes. He knows the exact number of hairs on your head and mine. He knows the location of every spider, snake and sparrow. We cannot comprehend all that He Is.

> "For My thoughts are not your thoughts, nor are your ways My ways," declares the Lord. "For as the heavens are higher than the earth, so are My ways higher than your ways, and My thoughts than your thoughts". *Isaiah 55:8-9*

CHAPTER 7

A Mother's Prayer

Cold rain fell one dark winter evening as the temperature plummeted to 14 degrees. I felt uneasy when I realized the roads were becoming very slippery. We lived in the country near Mt. Juliet, Tennessee. Our home was quite a ways from downtown Nashville where our son David was attending a night class at Belmont University.

David left the campus at eight o'clock that evening. He drove a new black Mustang, the car of his dreams. It was still an unfamiliar car to him and lightweight. Mustangs were not designed for traveling over icy roads. David had never attempted to drive on ice before; I knew he might be in for some trouble.

Our son began his trip home traveling east on Interstate 40. In a matter of minutes, he realized the Mustang was no match for the present road conditions.

I felt helpless each time he called with a progress report. The frozen roads were so treacherous that many cars could not even make it off the exit ramps. David had no choice but to continue eastward.

My husband and I prayed together and asked God to protect David and all the motorists who were out that night. Suddenly, I felt the urge to talk to God alone. I went into our bedroom and closed the door. I prayed, "Lord, You can do anything. Will You just melt the ice before him and bring David home safely tonight, please?"

When I arose, the fear was gone, and I had a certain knowledge that David should detour from his planned route. I had an inner peace that he should make his way toward Andrew Jackson Parkway. It was unlikely that road would be salted, but I knew what God imparted when I prayed.

David agreed to change his course as soon as he was able and I felt a sense of relief. From that moment on, Burke and I knew what we needed to do. He prepared the four-wheel-drive SUV for any foreseeable difficulties we might encounter then we drove toward David with great caution. We saw many cars in ditches, yet we moved slowly but surely along at a crawl.

We were pleasantly surprised when our son called to say he had managed to reach the hardware store in Hermitage. He said, "My car is in one piece, and I would like to leave it here in the parking lot."

When we arrived, David was happy to see us. The first thing he said was, "What a trip. I was glad to see the ice melted on Andrew Jackson Parkway. I was the only driver in sight, and I drove at normal speed. Water sprayed up from my tires as I drove."

We traveled home the same way we came, very slowly and on ice. We all knew it was not possible for ice to melt when the temperature was 14 degrees. It was not humanly possible for our son to drive at normal speed with water splashing on the side of his car that night. Nothing is impossible with God. That evening we received a reminder:

> *"With God all things are possible".*
> *Matthew 19:26*

I believe a merciful Heavenly Father heard a mother's prayer for her faithful son. He answered her prayer by sending exactly what she asked for. God melted the ice. God still receives the glory for that answered prayer each time we tell the story.

Our family made it home safely and we arrived in our warm, country kitchen where the embers glowed in the fireplace, inviting us to warm our cold hands. It was so good to be home; our family was safe and under one roof. God's Divine intervention demonstrated His love and His presence. Prayers of praise and thanksgiving overflowed from our hearts as we drifted off to sleep with the assurance that we were surely loved and safe in our Heavenly Father's care.

He (God) sends forth His command to the earth; His word runs very swiftly. He gives snow like wool; He scatters the frost like ashes. He casts forth His ice as fragments; who can stand before His cold? He sends forth His word and melts them [the ice]; He causes His wind to blow and the waters to flow.
Psalm 147:15-18

CHAPTER 8

The Vision

The summer of 1997 was an unforgettable one. June started out joyfully; however, it ended very sadly. Two families, who were close to our family, lost a child that June. One family lost a baby girl due to an infection, and a second family lost a son in a freak accident. The deaths brought back memories. A few years back, my little niece died when she drowned in a backyard pool. When there is death, there is always the pain of letting go. Each tragedy reminded us that children are the hardest ones to let go.

On a Saturday afternoon the last week of June, I was emotionally drained. My words of consolation spoken to grieving family members sounded as cold and empty as an echo in a canyon. How I wished I could ease some of the pain in the broken hearts of those people who had suffered such great loss. The loss and separation was so new that nothing could help them except the Lord. My heart ached for them.

The afternoon was ending when I retreated to a quiet room and closed the door. I needed to be alone with God to pray for those people. I lifted up each person along with their loss and prayed for relief from the suffering they were experiencing.

I remember saying, "Lord, You can do anything. You can touch them with the tip of Your finger and help them. Please do something for them. Father, won't You give them something to ease their pain and make them better." Honestly, I was not expecting an audible reply from the Lord. I was confused when I received such a reply. Immediately the Lord spoke softly, saying, "You give them something."

I was silent. I didn't know how to respond. After a reverent pause, I slowly replied, "Lord, I don't have anything to give them."

The Lord revealed an unsettling vision to me at that time. I saw an exhibition before me that resembled a scene on a movie screen. There was an endless sea of faces all wearing theatrical masks with downturned mouths and downturned eyes. They were crying out loudly, and their arms reached toward Heaven. The outcry of grief was deafening and distressing emotionally. The faces vanished from sight as suddenly as they appeared.

These words came next, "If you extract the precious from the worthless, you will become My spokesman." I recognized the Scripture from the Book of Jeremiah 15:19.

There in the stillness and quiet, I heard a song in my spirit and in my head. The lyrics and melody came at the same time. I captured the song on paper and mentally noted the melody. I remained quiet for several minutes but neither saw nor heard anything after that.

The feelings I had during those few minutes were unshakable in the days that followed. I realized I had heard from God but did not know what to make of it. Days later, I arranged for a friend to record the song. The faces, the cries, and the song stayed in my mind; it was disturbing.

I made an appointment with our pastor, and told him what I saw and heard. He listened to the song. He didn't know what to make of my experience either. As time passed, I acknowledged that God had declared a vision to me, but I did not understand the significance of it. God is a patient God. I have learned that many years may pass before we understand a message from Him.

As mentioned previously, in 2005, my husband, Burke, died at the age of 53. Minutes after he died, he appeared in the home of Dr. Carl Willis, in an after-death appearance. The night following his death, my husband appeared in the home of Dr. Arthur Cushman in an after-death appearance. Burke gave both of the doctors similar messages. The after-death appearances and messages were gifts of hope. The doctors shared their encounters with me.

The appearances to the two doctors and the messages my husband imparted were actually the inspiration that led me to write A Fax from Heaven and *Real Messages from Heaven*. These books offer hope and encouragement to those who have lost loved ones and to those who are uncertain about their Salvation. They clearly demonstrate there is life after death and there is a need to seek God while there is still time.

The experience of writing the books and being used by God as a tool reminded me of the Scripture from Jeremiah that I heard that night long ago. *"If you extract the precious from the worthless, you will become My spokesman."*

Death is the last enemy. When God allowed my husband to return with his message, God made it possible for a message of hope to be extracted from something as 'worthless' as death. God gave me the strength and ability to share that message. Could I possibly be considered His spokesperson, a vessel for His purpose? I wanted to help those who were devastated by death. By way of the books, I believe God is using me to help others. He told me, "You give them something." I believe God is giving them something through me.

It took 13 years for the vision to finally make sense. Then there is the matter of the song. I believe the song, Coattails of Jesus, is Burke's message to me from Heaven, although God imparted the words to me before my husband died. Perhaps the song is a message to each of us from our loved ones who are now in Heaven.

Coattails of Jesus

There are some things that I would say,
if I were there with you,
Like dry your eyes and rest your mind, some things we
can't undo.
I will always love you, we're apart for just a while,
don't forget, there are no tears,
in the presence of His smile.

The water in the river, of life never sleeps,
The banks are overflowing, with promises He'll keep.
So lift your head and look up, into a hope-filled sky,
Know that I'll be waiting, where we'll
never say good-bye.

I'm holding on, to the coattails of Jesus.

There's no chance of me letting go.

Inside the gates, there's no such thing as darkness,

No shadows in the Light that's white as snow.

Please go on believing in the reason

heaven sings,

It wasn't God who took my life,

but He gave me wings.

Last but not least, remind your heart to see,

you've not seen the last of me…

CHAPTER 9

Perfect Timing

When I awoke, the red digital numbers on the face of the clock glowed in the darkness; I distinctly recall the time read 4:44. I talked to the Lord until 5:30. At that particular time, I began praying for my daughter who was going through a flare-up of Sarcoidosis, a painful inflammatory disease that affects all major organs, including the eyes.

As I prayed, I thought of a conversation two years earlier with a woman who also suffered from Sarcoidosis. She had done extensive research on the disease and she learned much about available medical treatment. Most doctors have little experience treating Sarcoidosis, and the woman who came to mind possessed a wealth of potentially beneficial knowledge. I wanted to ask her some questions. I remembered her name was Kathy, but I could not remember her last name.

Kathy and I had spoken by phone, but we had never met. I could not even remember who put me in contact with her in the first place; I had no way of finding her. I spoke to the Lord about my desire to speak to Kathy and prayed, "Lord, if You want us to talk, You will have to have her call me."

Later that morning, I went to my daughter's home to take care of my young grandson. I answered the phone when it rang at 1:30 that afternoon. A voice said, "This is Kathy and I'm trying to reach Faye." The woman I had prayed to find only eight hours earlier had called my daughter's home to find me. Surprised that my prayer was answered so quickly, I asked her why she called and how she obtained my daughter's number. She said she was compelled to call me from the time she got out of bed that morning. Though not sure how to find me, she remembered the woman who put us in touch initially and gave her a call. The woman gave Kathy a phone number, not realizing it was actually my daughter's number. Kathy dialed the number and, lo and behold, I answered the phone at my daughter's house.

Kathy felt certain she was supposed to share the name of an ophthalmic solution with me. Since it had decreased her eye symptoms significantly, she thought it might be beneficial to my daughter. I told her about my prayer and we were both amazed at how God worked to connect us. He really does hear every prayer.

Some answers come swiftly and others take time, but He hears our earnest and sincere prayers.

At 5:30 that morning, while I was speaking to God, God was speaking to Kathy. He knew exactly where I would be at 1:30, so He provided Kathy with the number she needed to reach me at that precise time. God answered my prayer as I prayed.

God's ways are wonderful. Sometimes, I think He works in such ways to cause me to pause and look up." I can almost hear Him say, "Did you get that? Do you think there is anything I cannot handle? Do you realize I know your every thought, your every word, and your every prayer, even before you speak?" He can orchestrate circumstances and situations in ways that are impossible for us to understand. God works in mysterious ways.

Not long after that incident, I came across an interesting article from a newspaper about a well-known minister who was driving cross-country. The man needed some alone time with God so he decided to drive to his destination. He was hundreds of miles from his home when he stopped to rest and stretch his legs. He was walking past an outdoor pay phone when the phone started ringing. He looked around and no one else was nearby. He lifted the receiver and said 'Hello'.

He heard a woman's voice calling him by name. He was stunned into silence as he listened to her express how happy she was to reach him. She asked the minister if he was in his office and he replied, "No". He told the woman his location and asked how in the world she could possibly have reached him since no one knew exactly where he was.

The woman explained her desperate situation and her serious need to talk to him. She wanted the minister to pray for her. She had prayed to God, telling the Lord her desire to talk to the minister. She said a number 'suddenly appeared in her mind' so she dialed the number at once, thinking it must be his home or office number.

Both the minister and the caller were astonished when they realized how God had positively stepped in to answer her prayer as soon as the words left her mouth. The incident was undeniable proof of God's orchestration in the circumstances. Each of them learned a valuable lesson that day about the omnipotence of God, the power of prayer and the force of faith.

Be it done to you according to your faith. *Matthew 9:29*

CHAPTER 10

Healed

Donna Layne knew she served a miracle-working God. She and our family prayed for God to remove a large cyst that was located in the very back of her throat, in the pharynx.

The days and weeks passed and she experienced no noticeable change in her condition. The painful and annoying condition reminded her something was very wrong each time she spoke words or even swallowed food or water.

Donna scheduled an appointment with an ENT specialist. Dr. Reiber was a very personable man, and he seemed to be very knowledgeable in his field of expertise. He advised Donna to have an operation, allowing him to remove the cyst. She agreed to have the procedure.

Our daughter, Donna, and I met at the Surgery Center on the day of the operation. After registration, a nurse escorted Donna to the restricted surgery area beyond the lobby.

Perhaps an hour and a half passed before the surgeon appeared in the waiting room and approached me. He looked a bit confused, and he began to explain what just happened.

Dr. Reiber spoke in amazement, saying, "I went in to remove the cyst but it was gone. It was there, but it is not there now. She is waking up now, but she did not have surgery. Only an indentation remains, indicating something was once there. There is no need for surgery."

I voiced my thanks to God and expressed my faith to Dr. Reiber, telling him I believed in God's power to heal. I did not understand why God chose to heal sometimes and not always, but I trusted His authority and His judgment. Dr. Reiber agreed with me, yet he seemed to be a little puzzled. I suppose Dr. Reiber and I both knew God had used him to document and authenticate a miraculous healing.

Donna awoke, signed the necessary forms and walked out of the medical facility. It is amazing to witness God's extraordinary power when he intervenes and allows us to observe His actions.

Donna was aware the cyst existed when she arrived at the facility—the cyst vanished between the time she walked out of the lobby and the time she re-entered the lobby.

Each of us knew we had experienced something astonishing and supernatural. How very like God to validate His exceptional work about answered prayer by using an unsuspecting, scientifically minded physician as a witness. Many years have passed since that happened, but I clearly remember what an incredible experience that was.

> Oh Lord my God, I cried to You for
> help, and You healed me. *Psalm 30:2*

CHAPTER 11

Angel Food

Burke Aldridge grimaced from the pain of lung and bone cancer; he slowly opened his eyes as he tried to make sense of regaining consciousness on day 21 of hospitalization. His eyes surveyed the small hospital room. He was uncertain of his surroundings. I gently explained to Burke, telling him he had been moved from the Intensive Care Unit back to the Critical Care Unit at Baptist Hospital in Nashville. The room in CCU provided less human interference from medical personnel and more privacy for Burke and our family.

Burke had not eaten in two weeks; on the last Sunday afternoon of his life, he announced, "I want something to eat." Our son was present and exclaimed to his dad that he would go anywhere and find anything he desired. Burke said, "I only want a bite of something...

I wish I had a bite of a SNICKERS® candy bar and a bite of cantaloupe." The Lord provided for Burke that day by undeniable godly and divine intervention.

One bite of a SNICKERS® candy bar and one bite of cantaloupe was Burke's last earthly meal. He wanted no more and no less. Earlier that same day, our daughter, Donna, came to the hospital to see her dad and she brought fresh fruit for me to eat, which I did not eat. Fresh cantaloupe in a small, sealed container sat on a shelf near the sink. It took only seconds to grant half of Burke's request.

A family friend came to the hospital the day before to see Burke and brought a bag of snacks for me. I did not know what the bag contained; however, I caught a glimpse of the word SNICKERS® when I moved the bag from ICU to CCU the day before. Sure enough, the bag rendered a package of small SNICKERS® candy bars. Burke's request was fulfilled in less than a minute.

I did not think it was strange that God supplied Burke's last meal before we or he knew he wanted it. It was merely evidence of God's presence and personal touch. During those moments while David and I shared the food with Burke, I felt surrounded by the merciful and loving presence of a compassionate God. I knew without question that God was in the room with us.

To this day, when I think of cantaloupe or SNICKERS® candy bars, I think of angel food. God generously provided angel food for Burke that cold February day.

> Are not two sparrows sold for a cent? And yet not one of them will fall to the ground apart from your Father. But the very hairs of your head are all numbered. So do not fear; you are more valuable than many sparrows. Therefore everyone who confesses Me before men, I will also confess him before My Father who is in heaven. But whoever denies Me before men, I will also deny him before My Father who is in Heaven *Matthew 10:29-33*.

CHAPTER 12

Pray and Trust

In the winter of 1996, something unusual happened every day for two weeks. I awoke at four o'clock each morning and each time, I was strongly compelled to pray. Some mornings, I was startled awake. Other mornings, I felt a hand on my shoulder, gently shaking me. It was not a human hand. Each time I scrambled out of bed and obeyed the voice that was silent to my ears yet audible to my spirit.

My family and I lived in a wonderful, rambling farmhouse surrounded by 47 acres of trees and Tennessee wildlife. My husband and I claimed the downstairs part of the house while our son David claimed half of the upstairs area. That left a large area upstairs for our daughter, her husband, and their young son. Our son-in-law was still in college, so we encouraged them to share our home. We had more than enough space.

During that time, we were three generations under one roof, and I will always treasure the memories of that cherished era that has long since passed.

My pre-dawn prayer place was in the middle of the family room downstairs. When I began seeking the Lord at four o'clock each morning, I routinely lit a large candle in the center of the coffee table and knelt there. The early morning wake-up calls continued for a period of two weeks. The Lord did not tell me why I was to spend extra time with Him; He just imparted to me that I should pray, and I obeyed.

One evening, I was standing at the sink washing the dinner dishes when our son David came home from a night class at Belmont University. I looked over my shoulder at him, smiled, and said, "I'm glad you're home." He had a perplexed look on his face and his hand rested on his upper chest.

David said, "Something is wrong," indicating something was wrong in his upper chest area. Because David never complained, I knew he was experiencing a real problem. The look on his face, the sound of his voice, and the way he held his chest sent chills over me. I sensed a dark presence and the hair on the back of my neck literally stood up. The Bible tells us that 'Satan is the thief who comes only to steal, kill, and destroy'. I quieted the intruder by speaking the last part of that Scripture that says 'Jesus came so that we might have life and have it abundantly.' (See John 10:10.)

In my spirit, I heard the Lord saying, "This is why I wanted you to pray more than usual for the past two weeks. Your faith must be strong." I tried not to sound alarmed as I told David I would call our doctor in the morning and ask him to do an examination.

Dr. Seeley saw David the next day and scheduled a diagnostic study at Tennessee Medical Center in Madison, Tennessee, for the following day. David went straight from Belmont to the hospital for the test shortly after lunchtime.

I remember going through my day as usual when I was filled with the feeling that I really needed to go to the hospital. I dropped everything and drove straight there. The diagnostic study took a very long time when it should have taken no more than 30 minutes. When David appeared in the waiting room, he appeared unsettled. I asked the nurse if the test showed any abnormality, and she searched for the right words. She said, "You will have to talk with your doctor on

Monday." I questioned persistently, and the radiologist agreed to speak to me. He said the test showed a very large esophageal tumor. I thanked him, and we left the hospital and headed home.

Before I reached our home, the doctor called and said he had scheduled an appointment on Monday for David to see a gastroenterologist. He expressed the seriousness and the urgency of the situation. I thanked him and attempted to gather my thoughts so I could be in a good frame of mind when I got home.

Over the weekend, my husband and I prayed without ceasing, and I read and reread the Scriptures, especially the ones that promised God would heal if we only believe. I watched from the window as David pitched a ball to Jacob, our little grandson. The football ended up on top of the roof above the patio. David attempted to retrieve the ball by climbing out a second story window. I helped him remove the screen. I touched his back as he crawled inside through the window and, somehow, I knew at that moment God had healed David. I truly believed, but I needed confirmation.

On Monday, I accompanied David to the pre-arranged appointment with the gastroenterologist, and we listened as the doctor gave his opinion based on the esophagram results and the radiologist report. He advised us there was a chance the tumor would be malignant. He suggested a biopsy right away and advised us to have the anticipated operation done at Vanderbilt Medical Center in Nashville. The doctor said the surgery would alter David's life drastically. A section of the esophagus would be removed. This would necessitate pulling the upper stomach up to close the gap. A lifetime of medication and a special diet would follow. That was the good news. If it was cancer and if it had spread, those procedures would not help at all.

My brain tried to digest what the medical professional said, but my spirit said I should have no part of what he was saying. I asked him to schedule the biopsy for Friday, knowing that would give us a week to seek the Lord and wait for His guidance. I was aware of what the Bible taught us.

> *"Do not fear, for I am with you"* Isaiah
> *41:10.*

David was young, and I loved him so much. I could not bear the thought of an unnecessary surgical procedure. I prayed, saying, "Lord, I asked You to heal

David completely, causing the tumor to wither and cease to exist, and I believe You have healed him." The room was still dark, but I saw the face of a man appear before my eyes. The face disappeared in a few seconds. The face was hazy but I thought, I must know him. I said, "Lord, that face looked like Dr. Fox." I saw nothing else. I thought, "This doctor will give us confirmation that the tumor is gone."

Dr. Fox was a physician I met on one occasion in the past. I recalled he was a medical missionary earlier in his life. I searched the phone book and located his number. I called and talked with his office manager. I briefly explained our situation and I told her, "I know my son has been healed. Please see if Dr. Fox will examine him." Later that same day, David and I sat in Dr. Fox's office. I briefly explained our situation and my firm belief that God had healed David on Saturday. Dr. Fox understood, and he agreed to order a CT scan, which would confirm or deny that the healing had taken place.

Dr. Fox called Thursday morning with wonderful news. He said, "The CT scan revealed there is no tumor. It showed only a calcified, withered lymph node where the tumor was shown on the previous study." I was elated. God had healed our son. Dr. Fox even used the word "withered." That was the same word I had used when I prayed, asking God to cause the tumor to wither and cease to exist. I knew we had confirmation from God, letting us know He had heard our prayers and He had answered our prayers.

We canceled the Friday biopsy appointment. Our family engaged in a faith walk of prayer and believing. God required us to seek His face. We had to listen with a sensitive and obedient spirit, and then follow through on what He showed us. We had to trust God and proceed a little at a time. That is how God works sometimes.

We thanked the Lord, and gave Him the glory for healing David and teaching us to trust Him no matter what. God's divine intervention gave David the gift of life that day. May we never forget. Our Lord, once again, had shown us compassion, mercy, and love.

CHAPTER 13

Poppa Tall

When innocent, small children see angelic beings, how can we possibly doubt? My granddaughter, Reese Isabella, was a year and a half old when her beloved Poppa passed away after a brief illness. I recall watching the two of them together a month before his death. My husband, Burke, and Reese appeared to be the only two people in the room—and in the whole world for that matter.

Burke sat in a chair and played the guitar for Reese. He sang Little Red Caboose for her repeatedly at her request. Reese stood directly in front of him with a tiny hand on each knee. When the music stopped, Reese squealed and asked for more, "Sing, Poppa, sing. Play tar, Poppa." A "tar" was a guitar in Reese's world.

The music and laughter between them was a beautiful thing. Reese danced, laughed, and captivated the heart of the man she knew and loved as Poppa.

When the music was over, he picked Reese up and held her close; then Burke lifted her high above his head while she laughed until she was out of breath. Precious memories.

One month after that musical afternoon, my husband died at Baptist Hospital in Nashville on a Monday evening around midnight. I called our son and daughter and asked them to come to the hospital at once. I did not tell them Burke was dead until they arrived in the room where I waited for them with Burke's body.

My son's wife, Rhonda, later told me how she went in to check on Reese when our son, David, left that night. Reese always slept on her belly with her knees drawn underneath her body. That night was different. Rhonda quietly peered into the crib and discovered Reese was asleep on her back with her little head tilted back, chin and lips extended forward. Rhonda said she knew at that moment that Poppa was dead, that he had stopped off to kiss his lovely little granddaughter goodbye.

A few weeks later, David, Rhonda, and Reese were relaxing on their screened-in back deck when Reese began to laugh and point excitedly. Her tiny finger pointed to the top of a row of trees along the back property line. Reese laughed with joyful laughter and innocently exclaimed repeatedly, "Poppa tall. Poppa tall." She saw what the others could not see.

On more than one occasion, Reese's parents observed her sitting in the middle of the bed, laughing and talking to an invisible Poppa. Each time they watched in amazement as she jabbered in baby talk and carried on what appeared to be a one-sided conversation to the observer. Children under the age of two don't know how to lie or deceive. She saw what she saw as an innocent child and responded honestly and openly. She is older now and has no recollection of the incidents; however, we will always remember, with much love and appreciation to God for His remarkable gifts.

> "Thanks be to God for His indescribable gift." *Second Corinthians 9:15*

Clouds

Our youngest grandson, Daniel, was only six years old when his grandfather died the end of February in 2005. We celebrated Daniel's seventh birthday two weeks later. I will be very honest; it wasn't much of a celebration. My daughter, Donna, tried her best to carry on with a cake and party for little Daniel, but the smiles were all make-believe for Daniel's sake.

I watched Daniel that day because in addition to being brokenhearted, he acted in a peculiar manner. He walked through the house peering into each room and into closets. He spoke words just above a whisper, and I could not tell what he was saying. I began to walk closely behind him, and I listened carefully to his words. He appeared to be playing hide and seek, a game he and Poppa played many times.

When I realized what he was saying each time he looked into a new possible hiding spot, my heart broke for that dear little boy. Daniel's eyes searched everywhere as he softly spoke, saying, "Poppa, you can come out now. It's my birthday, Poppa; please come out now." I thought my heart would break that day, and I am sure Daniel felt the same way. Hugs, kisses, and the words "I love you" were all I could give him. I am sorry to say I fell short of consoling him in a significant way. Sometimes we as humans have nothing to give in times of grief except our presence. In those terrible times, it is important to remember that God is with us.

Springtime appeared slowly that year. The green rye grass, yellow buttercups, and purple hyacinths pushed their heads out of the cold ground and the sunshine offered glimpses of hope that our world was still turning. I remember one warm day in late March when Daniel was visiting me at the farm. He played on his little green tractor under the carport as I worked in the kitchen.

Suddenly, I heard Daniel calling to me. Mothers and grandmothers can tell by the tone of voice if a shout is one about pain, fear, or excitement. Daniel's shout was all about excitement. He shouted for me to come quickly. I heard him say something about the sky. I hurried outside to find him standing firmly planted and pointing toward a sky of blue. Daniel told me to "Look." and I did.

To my astonishment, I saw the word LOVE in the beautiful blue sky. Each letter hung in the sky in the form of a billowy, white cumulous cloud. I became as excited as Daniel. Could this really be? Yes, it was very real. Both of us witnessed it. The letters began to lose shape almost as soon as I realized we were not dreaming. "And the witness in the sky is faithful" (Ps. 89:37).

A gentle breeze caught the letters and swept them into one large, fluffy cloud. A Heavenly Artist was at work. In Daniel's seven-year-old mind, his Poppa was saying, "I love YOU, Daniel." Daniel needed that more than anything that day. Who else but God could offer that sweet child love and hope from the heavens above? That was an amazing display of compassion and extraordinary love unlike anything I had ever seen.

According to the Bible, God manifests His holy presence in the clouds. He certainly did that day.

...When they praised the Lord saying, "He indeed is good for His lovingkindness is everlasting," then the house, the house of the Lord, was filled with a cloud, so that the priests could not stand to minister because of the cloud, for the glory of the Lord filled the house of God. *2 Chronicles 5:13-1*

CHAPTER 15

Stay for Now

It was the day after Christmas when I became ill. At the time, I lived alone in our home on a large piece of farmland. I had recently updated the kitchen with granite countertops and new appliances. The kitchen looked wonderful, so I decided to redo the paint on the walls myself. I worked for days standing on a tall ladder with my neck turned at an awkward angle. I painstakingly painted the trim, and it took a very long time. I am a perfectionist, so I painted and repainted until I was exhausted. The kitchen looked so pretty that I decided to paint the great room and the foyer too. I did not use good judgment when I decided to do the painting. I was forced to abandon my efforts and call a professional painter to finish the job.

When I awoke the day after Christmas, I could hardly stand up. My head and neck ached. I could hardly breathe and I was very dizzy. I painted most of the house without proper ventilation and the paint fumes affected me adversely. I thought a little rest would make me better, so I went back to bed.

My condition did not improve with time and rest. In early January, I went to my physician when my symptoms grew worse. I was extremely ill and weak. I did not want to alarm my family, but honestly, I thought it might be time to go home to Heaven. My husband died the year before and I really wanted to go and be with him. As a child of God, I did not fear dying. Heaven became more inviting by the minute.

On the 27th day of January, I went to bed wondering where I would wake up. Something extraordinary happened that night.

I was lying in bed, resting quietly in the darkened room. Suddenly, I saw my deceased husband, Burke, in an expanse in front of me. It seemed like I was looking inside a very large building through an invisible wall. He looked at me, and then moved beyond my sight. In a few moments, Burke was standing clearly in front of me only 10 or 12 feet away. I left my bed, and I did not walk to get to him—I stepped into his world for a brief time.

I was suddenly there, and I do not understand how I got there.

Burke wore a white shirt with short sleeves and cut-off blue jeans. That is what he usually wore when he cut the grass, and that is what he wore that night. I hugged him, and he hugged me. I felt his warm cheek against my cheek. His face was warm to touch and his body was solid matter. He felt no different to touch than he did when he was alive on earth.

My face was against his face when he spoke to me saying, "Love you, love you, love you." Burke always signed greeting cards he gave me that way. Perhaps that was his way of letting me know it was really him. I was startled and delighted to hear his voice, and I pulled my face back and looked into his eyes. His dark brown eyes sparkled. His smile was radiant as he looked at me intently. He was the picture of perfect health, peace, and happiness. I felt like all was right in the world once more.

I said to him, "May I go with you?" Burke replied, "You have to stay for now, for the children." I blinked my eyes, and I was back in bed inside my body. That is exactly what happened, but I cannot explain how it happened. I believe I died and left my body for a brief period then returned to my body. The experience was real. I was wide awake when the experience began and when it ended.

I clearly received God's message. He sent it through Burke with an encouraging and affectionate hug. I experienced God's love, kindness, and compassion firmly—yet in all His gentleness. I knew I had to get better and stay on earth to accomplish my purpose. I knew God had plans for me and plans for my life. The following weeks were difficult, but I steadily regained my strength and fully recovered.

One year later, I wrote my first book in order to share the incredible stories of my husband's after-death appearances. My first book was A FAX FROM HEAVEN and my second book was, REAL MESSAGES FROM HEAVEN. I have been writing ever since then, always attempting to give glory to God for all He has done. It is my sincere desire to share with others the very real power of faith, hope and God's love.

CHAPTER 16

White Feathers

I hugged my 16-year-old grandson just before he left the church and handed him a BP gas card. Jacob owned his very first car and had been driving for less than a week. He grinned and thanked me. Jacob kissed me on the cheek before he drove away that morning on his way to see his girlfriend.

After attending early service, I went into my Sunday school room for class. After class, a young woman ran to me and said, "Jacob has been in an accident. Have you heard?" My heart skipped a beat, and I ran to my car to find my phone.

I learned that Jacob was traveling on an unfamiliar road in search of a BP gas station when the accident occurred. Jacob in his car and a woman in her car both arrived at an intersection at precisely the same moment.

They were traveling at speeds of approximately 45 miles per hour when they crashed. The collision totaled both vehicles. Each car contained one occupant, the driver. Only by God's grace, each driver walked away from the accident without a scratch.

Jacob's mom, Donna, arrived at the scene of the accident shortly after it happened. My daughter hugged her son and looked him over, making certain he was all right. She looked at Jacob's demolished Volvo in horror. The safety airbag deployed on impact.

My grandson said, "Mom, I never knew airbags were filled with feathers."

Donna replied, "There are no feathers in airbags. They are filled with air. Why do you think they are filled with feathers?"

"When I crashed, I saw white feathers all around me. White feathers surrounded me and they were all over the seat." Jacob exclaimed.

Donna said the peace of God, which surpasses all comprehension, filled her at that moment.

> And the peace of God, which surpasses all comprehension, will guard your hearts and your minds in Christ Jesus. *Philippians 4:7*

Donna explained to Jacob, "Since you started driving, I have been praying for God to keep you safe, and each day I plead the blood of Jesus over you—and I claim the 91st Psalm over you."

> He who dwells in the secret place of the Most High shall abide under the shadow of the Almighty. I will say of the Lord, "He is my refuge and my fortress; my God, in Him I will trust."...He shall cover you with His feathers, and under His wings you shall take refuge....For He shall give His angels charge over you, to keep [guard] you in all your ways. *Psalm 91:1-2, 4, 11 NKJV*

Jacob jokingly but truthfully remarked, "So angels really do have feathers. White feathers." Jacob was amazed when he realized God's hand of protection had surely saved him and the other driver. The presence of the white feathers seemed to stress the fact that God wanted Jacob to remember who saved him.

Upon further inspection of the car, Jacob's mom noticed a small crushed section in the lower passenger side of the windshield. It appeared that a passenger's head had landed there, except for the fact there was no passenger. Jacob and our family believe an angel was riding with him at the time of the crash and for that, we are forever grateful to God.

CHAPTER 17

He Showed Me the Way

I backed my SUV out of the garage hurriedly and drove toward Mt. Juliet, Tennessee. I was supposed to visit a Women's Club meeting at Lake Providence Del Webb Community that day. I was running late, and five minutes into the trip, I realized I did not have the directions to where I was going. I knew the name of the street for the first left turn, but that was all I remembered.

I drove and I prayed. I did not get upset. I talked to the Lord as I made my way through traffic, not really knowing what I was going to do. When I came to the recognizable turn off the main road, I laughed aloud and spoke audibly to the Lord, "Lord, I know Kenny Martin is the guest speaker at the meeting today. It would really be great if You would send Kenny to show me the way."

I heard no reply but at that precise moment, my eyes were literally drawn to the tag on a black SUV ahead of me. My eyes felt like metal drawn to a magnet. I could not read the tag, so without taking my eyes off the tag; I accelerated and closed the distance between the two vehicles. When I got close enough to read the letters on the tag, I was overjoyed. The letters on the tag were the abbreviation for Mt. Juliet Chamber of Commerce. All I had to do was play follow the leader.

Kenny Martin worked as the Economic and Community Development Director for the City of Mt. Juliet at the time. I knew Kenny had to be one of the two men in that black SUV in front of me. As soon as I asked, my Heavenly Father answered "OK." He did exactly what I asked Him to do.

I followed the SUV to the security gates at Lake Providence. When the driver stopped for the security guard to check the guest list, I lowered my window and said to the guard, "I'm going where they're going." He waved me through; I know he wondered why I was laughing, especially since I appeared to be alone. I am never alone. God was with me, and I expect He was laughing too.

Kenny and his companion parked in the same area where I parked. I followed them to the clubroom.

When should we pray? If it matters to you or me, it matters to God. I believe our prayers are music to God's ears.

> Pray without ceasing; in everything give thanks; for this is God's will for you in Christ Jesus. *First Thessalonians 5:17-18*

CHAPTER 18

Holy Water

Michael Griffin, a close family friend and neighbor, often helped me at our farm after my husband, Burke, passed away. In early spring, my large mower required servicing. Michael and I talked as he prepared to load the mower onto his trailer. Michael was very fond of Burke and we reminisced about some of the happy times they shared.

As Michael prepared to leave, he flashed a big grin before he proudly told me the news. He and his wife, Alison, were expecting their first child.

That exciting news reminded me of the dream I had the night before, and I said to Michael, "I dreamed of Burke last night and in the dream, he mentioned your baby. I had no idea Alison was pregnant." I asked Burke, "What are you doing here?" He replied, "I've come to bring holy water for Michael's baby."

My deceased husband spoke those words as we stood in a vast dining room filled with men and women who appeared to be between the ages of 30 and 40 years old. They were all smiling and appeared to be genuinely happy as they engaged in lively conversations.

I finished speaking and I looked at Michael. He stood very still, with a curious look on his face. After a long pause, Michael spoke, saying, "We received a bottle of holy water for the baby from a family friend three days ago. It came in the mail."

I felt a tingling sensation flow up and down my arms, as if the hairs were standing on end. I realized something out of the ordinary was happening and something supernatural had already happened in the dream. Something supernatural also occurred to get the holy water from Lourdes, France' to a small town in Tennessee. Burke's after-death appearance in the dream could only mean the holy water was Heaven-sent for a specific reason.

In the after-death visit, Burke spoke of holy water for Michael's baby. Burke knew about the baby before I did although he was in Heaven. The fact that he mentioned holy water for the unborn baby was very significant.

Michael confirmed the significance when he announced the news about the pregnancy and the bottle of holy water they received three days earlier. Michael was taken aback that my deceased husband had already informed me about the baby and the holy water.

There was no way I could have known those two facts unless the knowledge came by way of Heaven in a genuine visit from my deceased husband. The dream was a real visit.

Almost three years passed before Michael and I talked about the holy water incident again. Michael and Alison's healthy baby had grown into a healthy toddler. The child appeared to possess intelligence and perception well beyond his years. Rosy cheeks, soft red curls rimming his tiny face, and an angelic smile melted my heart each time I saw him.

One day, I decided to discuss the holy water dream with Alison and she told me an interesting story about her pregnancy. Alison suggested that I talk to her friend, Maggie Dyer of Gilbertsville, Pennsylvania. Maggie was the woman who sent the holy water. I asked Maggie what prompted her to mail the holy water from Lourdes for the baby. Maggie sent the holy water after a conversation with Alison's mom, Diane, who expressed concern for the unborn baby. An ultrasound report indicated the possibility of an abnormality with one kidney and the heart. Michael had not mentioned the abnormalities at the time of our conversation.

Alison, Diane and Maggie prayed that God would heal the baby and Alison decided to accept the baby as God gave him; he would be perfect in her eyes, no matter what. Alison rubbed the water on her stomach as Maggie suggested and she believed her baby was healed.

The baby was born in July and he arrived in good health, normal and perfect in every way.

God is not far from us. He hears every whispered prayer. He went to great lengths to send a message by a deceased person from Heaven and to send holy drops of water from France to Pennsylvania to Tennessee for a miraculous healing of a precious baby the doctors referred to as "a fetus."

> (God said,) *Before I formed you in the womb, I knew you… Jeremiah 1:5*

NOTE: Sick people have traveled to Lourdes, France, since 1858, when a young French girl, acting in obedience to visions she had of the Virgin Mary, dug a hole in the earth, releasing a miraculous spring that produced healing water. The initial few drops of water multiplied until a spring emerged. When the nuns at Lourdes bathed the sick and dying in the water, they got well. Millions of visitors go to Lourdes each year in search of the holy water, associated with thousands of supernatural cures over the years.[2]

2

CHAPTER 19

Saved

My father was only twenty-five years old when he began experiencing unusual debilitating symptoms. He was a very active man. His employment required strenuous physical outdoor exertion. He pushed himself to keep working as long as he could because he was the only wage earner in the family.

In November 1953, the time came when Daddy could not get out of bed one morning. He retained so much fluid that he could not even make a fist with his hands nor bend his legs at the knees. His face became very swollen and he had difficulty seeing because the tissue around his eyes became terribly swollen, almost forcing his eyes shut.

Our family lived in a small farming community in Holmes County, Mississippi. As a last resort, Dad was taken to a small hospital for emergency treatment. A general practitioner, Dr. Roy L. Smith, treated him at the hospital and admitted him for testing and treatment.

Each day, Dad grew sicker and more swollen despite efforts by his doctor to make him better. All signs indicated he was dying. Each day, friends visited my father in his room and many of them told him about God and Heaven. He knew he could not continue to live in his condition. He began looking forward to seeing those who visited each day with their Bible stories that gave him hope. He remarked one day, "I didn't come to the hospital to be sick. I came here to have church."

My mom was at a disadvantage because she had to care for three small children miles away. She did not have access to a phone or a car and she could only go to the hospital when she could get a ride there. It was an incredibly difficult time for the young wife and mother who had to assume all the care and responsibility for her family under those dire circumstances.

Dad's Aunt Louise, the wife of a minister, lived in another town many miles away. Louise offered to come and stay with Dad for several days. While she attended to her nephew, Louise McNeer made it her business to share the gospel of Jesus Christ with him and Daddy accepted Jesus.

One night in early December, Dad's condition declined rapidly. His kidneys stopped functioning and he realized he was dying. There was no cure for his disease and Dialysis was still unheard of in those days. Kidney failure meant certain death.

Dr. Smith was a compassionate man. He stayed in the room with Dad and Louise as the time of death neared. Penicillin was a relatively new drug at the time and Dr. Smith administered a Penicillin injection to his patient not really knowing if it would help at all. Minutes later, Dad's lips began swelling and he complained of difficulty breathing.

He experienced a severe allergic reaction to the Penicillin that actually hastened his death and shortened his time of suffering.

Dad told Dr. Smith, "It's feels like I am under a heavy cloud and I can't breathe because the cloud is pressing down against my chest."

Dr. Smith replied compassionately, "Don't worry, I promise you that cloud is about to lift and you will be able to breathe in just a minute."

Louise asked my dad, "Can you see Jesus yet?"

He replied, "Yes, I see Jesus, He is right there, can't you see Him? He's right here in front of me." Daddy died moments later, while looking into the face of Jesus by his own admission. Dr. Smith and Louise did not see anyone else in the room but both of them believed the dying man saw the Lord.

My parents had three children and I was the youngest child. I was one year old when he died. I did not know the story about my dad's conversion until I became an adult. I went to work for a general practitioner in Durant, Mississippi named Dr. Roy L. Smith.

Late in the afternoon, we usually experienced a lull in the flow of patients. When that happened, Dr. Smith frequently came into my office with a cup of coffee. He ordinarily sat in a chair near the front of my desk and each day, he told me a story. He served in the U S Army and was one of the courageous soldiers that stormed the Beaches of Normandy in World War II. Sometimes, he shared a war story with me. Other times, he shared accounts of patients he had cared for during his many years of medical practice.

One day Dr. Smith sat quietly, looking out the window, and then he began his story. I enjoyed hearing what he had to say and I respected and admired him very much. Dr. Smith began by saying, "One time, I had a patient and his last name was Moss. Can't remember his first name. He was just a boy." Dr. Smith knew me only by my married name. I said nothing to indicate to him that my maiden name was Moss and he continued.

"The man was as sick as he could be and he stayed in the hospital quite a while before he died. He had chronic Pyelonephritis. I gave him a shot of Penicillin one night, thinking it might help him. Didn't know he was allergic to it but he was. The Penicillin actually killed him but it was a blessing in disguise. He was dying a slow and miserable death, and he just died a little quicker after the Penicillin shot. I spent the evening with him, because I knew he was close to death."

Dr. Smith went on to tell me about the cloud my dad saw and how Jesus came for him. He said, "His Aunt led him to Christ."

I said nothing until Dr. Smith finished telling me all the details. At that time, I told him his patient was my father. I remember Dr. Smith's face frowned a little and he was silent. After a long pause, he looked at me and said, "You don't say." That was one of his familiar phrases. I nodded my head, yes. I assured him I was glad to know what really happened.

Looking back, God's hand guided me to go to work for that doctor or I would never have known about Dad's conversion experience. I visited my Great Aunt Louise much later in life and she gave me her account of Dad's last days. Dr. Smith has gone on to be with God now. I miss seeing that sweet man who shared so many of his memories with me.

Divine intervention led me to work for Dr. Smith so I could learn about my father's last minutes on earth. God wanted me to know what happened. I have no memory of my dad but I have the knowledge that he was saved. With that knowledge, came God's assurance that I will meet my dad one day in heaven.

> I trust in You, O Lord, I say, "You are my God." My times are in Your hands…Let Your face shine on Your servant, save me in Your unfailing love.
> *Psalm 31:14- 16*

CHAPTER 20

Jack

PART I

While sitting at my desk one day in late autumn of 2010, I worked but felt annoyed. I was concerned about a serious matter involving a friend. He was extremely intelligent, likeable, successful, and stubborn. He was gifted in many ways but he failed to see the significance of surrendering his life to Jesus. After his conversion, I believed he would be a spiritual giant, leading many souls to Christ. His circle of influence was vast.

By way of the Holy Spirit, I knew the Lord wanted to bless this individual, using him in a manner similar to the manner in which He used the Apostle Paul in biblical days. I had explained that to my friend on previous occasions. Paul was converted and changed from Saul to Paul. After his conversion, Paul lived life only for the glory of God, persuading others to follow Jesus. I believed God was using me as one willing to witness to and pray for the man I often referred to as 'reluctant Paul'. I had stood in the gap for several years, praying and believing for his true conversion. My faith was intact but I was impatient and eager to see my prayers answered; to see visible changes in 'Paul'.

I completed the story I was working on and felt strongly that I should close that story with a verse of Scripture. The Scripture was Philippians 4:7 and I recalled the words to the Scripture but not the address. I typed these words: "And the peace of God, which surpasses all comprehension, will guard your hearts and your minds in Christ Jesus."

I wanted to get the words down correctly so I double-checked. I looked in my Bible concordance and located the Scripture address. I closed the concordance and reached for my Bible. I opened the Bible with one motion and the Scripture was immediately before my eyes. I did not look for it or thumb through pages. One turn of my wrist, and I read the words from the Bible that I just typed on my keyboard then read from my computer screen.

I thought to myself, God surely caused that to happen. Before I finished that thought, the phone rang. I answered and heard a pre-recorded message from a prayer ministry[3]. The voice said, "Pray for the peace that surpasses all comprehension…" I recalled how the Apostle Paul, by way of the Holy Spirit, wrote The Book of Philippians. Through divine intervention, the Holy Spirit was bolstering my faith and encouraging me by echoing the Apostle Paul's words to me in reference to the 'Paul' for whom I was praying.

When the call ended, I thought, God is so amazing. My left hand is still on the Bible and my finger is pointing to the same words. My right hand rested on the phone receiver God used to echo the words into my ears. My eyes stared at the same words on the computer screen. I received one Scriptural affirmation multiple ways in less than two minutes.

I recalled the matter over which I was aggravated only moments before. I was impatient and frustrated with my friend for resisting God and I was wrong to allow those feelings. My emotions were actually expressions of doubt. Faith will not work when there is doubt. I realized that God cared about my friend and knew exactly how and when to reach him.

I believed, by faith, that God would settle the matter His way and in His time. I said to the Lord, "I will never give up. I will pray and trust You, Lord, until You answer my prayers."

I thought to myself; how many of life's failures are people who did not realize how close they were to success when they gave up?

> "My righteous one shall live by faith. If he shrinks back, My soul has no pleasure in him. We are not of those who shrink back to destruction, but of those who have faith to the preserving of the soul."
> *Hebrews 10:38-39*

PART 2

Another year passed and still, no answer to my persistent prayers. I was praying one day in January and I expressed to the Lord that I really needed some kind of encouragement in the matter. I am sorry to say that I am impatient by nature. I did something

I do oftentimes when praying. I asked the Lord for a sign by a particular month, date and year. The date I clearly specified was March 1, 2012.

On March 1, 2012, I sat in my chair at my desk working on an interesting project. I heard the phone ringing and allowed the answering device to receive the call because I did not want to be interrupted.

I listened to the message a short time later and was surprised and humbled by the message. The message was from the same ministry I spoke of earlier in this chapter. The recorded voice of Dr. Charles Stanley made a clear statement. I suppose the message applied to many circumstances for others as well; however, it certainly applied to my specific prayer in which *I asked for an answer by a certain time*. I understood that God was speaking through Dr. Stanley. Here are the words that Dr. Stanley spoke.

"Sometimes we're impatient with God. We often react this way when God seems silent or slow about answering our concerns. We should know better. Scripture makes it clear that our sovereign and loving Heavenly Father always acts on behalf of those who trust Him. That is why it is never wise to trust in our limited strength and understanding. Instead, *release any deadlines you have placed on God.* Be still in the presence of the Lord and wait patiently for Him to act, because all the time, He is readying circumstances, shielding you from danger, purifying your motives, and drawing you closer to Him. Looking back on my own life, I remember how many times God has said to me, 'Just trust Me. I'm going to be on time. I'm not going to miss any details; I'll give you My very best.' I have always found His promise to be true. Wait upon the Lord and you will experience life at its' very best." [4]

Once again, the Lord used Dr. Stanley to speak to me about the same person and the same prayer. God placed the desire in me to pray for the accomplishment of the difficult task. With His involvement, I knew I would be able to keep the faith. I still believe my friend is a chosen vessel and God will have His way with him at the perfect time. I believe 'Paul' will lead many, many souls to Christ. Time will surely tell.

Can't the same great wonders be done today that were done many years ago? Where is the God of Elijah? He is waiting for today's Elijah to call on Him.

4

The greatest Old or New Testament saints who ever lived were on a level that is quite within our reach. The same spiritual force that was available to them and the energy that enabled them to become our spiritual heroes are also available to us. If we exhibit the same faith, hope, and love they exhibited, we will achieve miracles as great as theirs. A simple prayer from our mouths will be powerful enough to call down from heaven God's gracious dew or the melting fire of His Spirit, just as the words from Elijah's mouth called down literal rain and fire. All that is required is to speak the words with the same complete assurance of faith with which he spoke. –by Dr. Goulburn, Dean of Norwich. [5]

And the Lord's bond servant must not be quarrelsome, but be kind to all, able to teach, patient when wronged, with gentleness, correcting those who are in

5

opposition,   if perhaps God may grant them repentance leading to the knowledge of the truth. Second Timothy 2:24-25

Part 3

On July 2, 2024, Jack Lowery, aka, 'Paul', and I sat at my kitchen table. We finished our noon meal and lingered there;   reminiscing about our uncommon friendship that had endured since December 15, 2008. Time is fleeting and we touched on that truth. Jack had recently celebrated his 88th birthday.   Perhaps,   considering the brevity of life was what gave Jack pause.

Suddenly and miraculously, the Holy Spirit moved in Jack's heart; prompting him to call on God. Reverently, Jack bowed his head in submission and prayed a heartfelt prayer. He surrendered his life to Jesus Christ.

It was the end of an era and the beginning of a brand new life.

The Light has always been at the end of the tunnel. It just takes some of us longer than others to see it.

End Notes

1. St. John of the Cross, DARK NIGHT OF THE SOUL (Orlando, Florida 32822: Bridge Logos Publishers 2007) Used by permission.

2. www.lourdescenter.org/lourdeswater.html

3. Dr. Charles Stanley, In Touch Ministry, Prayer Partners Recorded Messages, Ministry, Atlanta, Georgia

4. Dr. Charles Stanley, In touch Ministry, Prayer Partners Recorded Messages, Ministry, Atlanta, Georgia

5. L.B. Cowan, Streams in the Desert, p 222, Zondervan Publishers, Grand Rapids, MI 49530 Used by permission.

Made in the USA
Columbia, SC
20 September 2024

42228054R00079